William Young

Lights and shadows of New York picture galleries

William Young

Lights and shadows of New York picture galleries

ISBN/EAN: 9783742860507

Manufactured in Europe, USA, Canada, Australia, Japa

Cover: Foto ©Thomas Meinert / pixelio.de

Manufactured and distributed by brebook publishing software
(www.brebook.com)

William Young

Lights and shadows of New York picture galleries

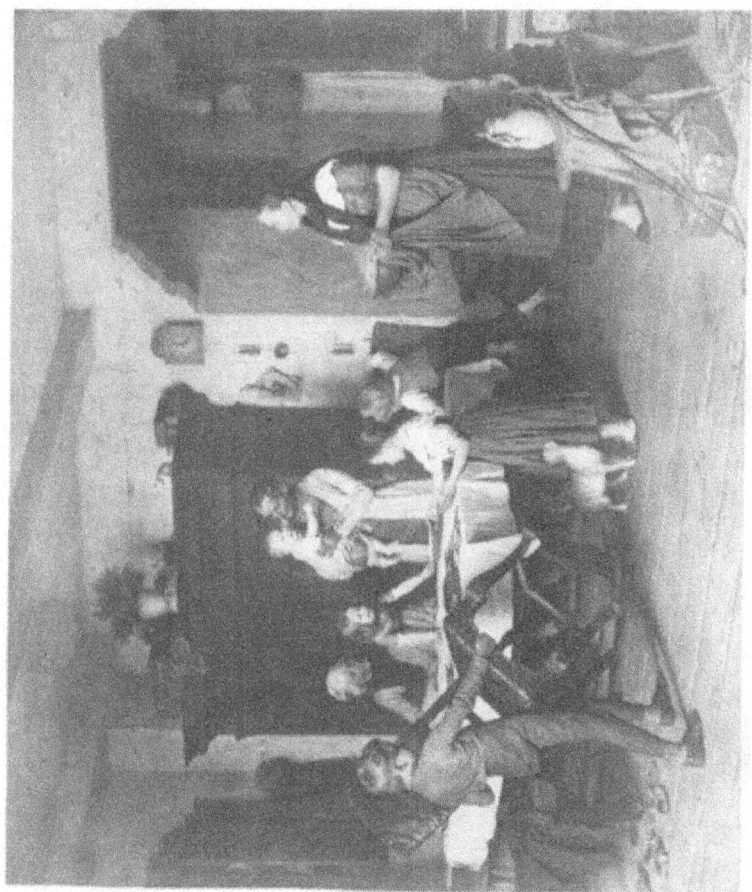

LIGHTS AND SHADOWS

OF

NEW YORK PICTURE GALLERIES.

FORTY PHOTOGRAPHS, BY A. A. TURNER,

SELECTED AND DESCRIBED BY

WILLIAM YOUNG.

Mislike me not for my complexion,
The shadowed livery of the burning sun!
Merchant of Venice, Act II, Scene I.

NEW YORK:
D. APPLETON AND COMPANY, 443 & 445 BROADWAY.
LONDON: 16 LITTLE BRITAIN.
1864.

PREFACE.

A few prefatory words appear to be needful, in reply to an anticipated enquiry—why are not all the Photographs in this collection of equal excellence?

The answer is simple. As with Nature; so with Pictures. The process is not yet invented, by which the delicate operations of Photography can be made independent of colour. Furthermore, there is a peculiar difficulty in the attempt to copy paintings in oil, caused by the varying chemical properties of the pigments employed, and of the varnish with which they are overlaid. Beyond this, again, there is the differing condition, to which time and exposure may have brought the work. It follows therefore that, as no two originals are similarly adapted for the purpose desired, so no two transcripts can be precisely alike in fidelity and effect. And it follows also, that it is impossible to measure accurately the merit of any Picture, here reproduced, by the clearness or delicacy or strength—or, in short, by the general success, with which it has now been copied.

To the gentlemen who have—liberally, and often at inconvenience to themselves—lent their treasures, in order that they may be thus popularized, the Publishers desire to express their grateful thanks. The promptness, with which the favour was accorded, shows that the genuine lover of Art for its own sake retains his interest therein, amid the tumult of a civil war and the pressure of high political excitement.

New York, *25th November*, 1863.

CONTENTS.

THE PEASANTS' REPAST

F. E. MEYERHEIM.

IN THE GALLERY OF **AUGUST BELMONT, ESQ.**

The domestic affections of the worthy Germans appear to be nourished, to some extent, by universal interest in things pertaining to the flesh. Go into the house of a wealthy merchant, anywhere between Rotterdam and Frankfort, and you are pretty sure to find prominent places on the walls assigned to Burgomasters—in oil and on canvas —carousing with their wives and daughters, or to ladies in purple and fine linen holding earnest consultation with their cooks. In this instance, it is true, there is not much show of luxurious entertainment; and the group that clusters round the table, in expectation of the good dame's smoking dish, is chiefly distinguished by the happy accord that prevails. The three generations have evidently been used to dwell together in harmony. The grandsire holds on his knee a little favorite, who clamours for her plate without fear of being scolded. The father pets the youngest of his brood. They have simple manners, these honest folk. There is not a semblance of constraint anywhere. You can almost hear the kitten purring, either in unison with the general home feeling, or as sniffing in anticipation a possible morsel.

Not ranging with the highest-class works conspicuous in this Gallery, this one—out of the many scores of its kind thrown off annually by German and Flemish artists—owes its place here to the favour of the sun, who is no respecter of painters' reputations. The finest Teniers or Gerard Douw might, like Malvolio in "Twelfth Night," have "been yonder i' the sun, practising behaviour to his own shadow, this half-hour," and yet come out a blotched and unsatisfactory reproduction. On the other hand, artists, greatly their inferiors, are sometimes far more fortunate in this respect. To what degree this is notable in this particular instance, there is no occasion to decide; in the words of Falstaff: "We have a number of shadows to fill up the muster-book"—and this is one of them.

IDLE DOGS.

E. VERBOECKHOVEN.

IN THE GALLERY OF WILLIAM P. WRIGHT, ESQ.

SOME one has pleasantly remarked that the dog—he, at least, of the sporting genus —is a natural-born gentleman, so difficult is it to train him to any industrious pursuit save that which tallies with his own instincts, so keenly and indefatigably does he enter into the excitement of following out his own good will. Adopting this conceit, and pushing it a little further, one might suppose our gentlemen, as here portrayed, not averse to the lounging of Club life.

But if each of these animals could tell his lineage and relate his exploits in the field, the story might perhaps be worth setting down. You would like to know, for instance, what fur or feathers there may be remaining in that up-hung game-bag, the flavour of which still has attraction for the sharp-visaged fellow rising on tiptoe, and for the inquiring nose of his comrade, also a-foot. You would like to know, moreover—the dog-lore of Continental Europe not being so familiar as that of England—to what breed each individual belongs.

Not unlike in build and figure, the two that stand are totally dissimilar in the head, there where the varying traits of the canine races are most distinctly marked. The one with fine-drawn muzzle and pointed ears, that cranes upward to satisfy his curiosity in the matter of the game-bag, reminds you of an Irish lurcher or a Russian grey-hound; though, if he have affinity with either, you can scarcely account for this development of the scenting instinct—the grey-hound and the lurcher hunting by sight. In the other, certain characteristics of the setter cannot be mistaken.

But whatever the genealogy or the sporting capabilities of this brace, and of their drowsy partners in the group, the subject forms a pleasant change from the rams and ewes and lambs, with which that popular artist, Verboeckhoven, is usually associated in the amateur's recollection. The picture is a very small one, delicate in handling, pleasant in tone, and finished with minutest care.

u

THE FLOWER-GIRL.

C. C. INGHAM.

IN POSSESSION OF JONATHAN STURGES, ESQ.

It might perhaps be more appropriate to entitle this subject: "A Girl Offering **Flowers for Sale**," seeing that there is next to nothing about it indicative of the calling or its exercise. Yet the profession is a tolerably old one, if Bulwer Lytton may be trusted, in whose "Last Days of Pompeii" the fair young Thessalian slave Nydia added the charm of a musical voice to the beauty of her wares, as she sang thus of her "children of the Earth":

> They are fresh from her lap I know;
> For I caught them, fast asleep
> In her arms, an hour ago,
> With the air which is her breath—
> Her soft and delicate breath:—
> Over them murmuring low.

In modern times and in Continental Europe, every large city, from Stockholm to Palermo and from Cadiz to Pesth, has, without doubt, its local race of flower-girls. **Those of Florence** have been often celebrated in prose and verse.

It would seem to be otherwise in Pennsylvania, where Mr. Ingham met his original and sketched her from life. Even without the aid of colour, laid on with the refinement and elaboration of finish that characterize all this artist's works, there is a certain charm about the young person; yet little—as already hinted—to remind you of her vocation. The costume indicates nothing whatever; the action scarcely more. In it there is no echo of the invitation,

> Come, buy! come, buy! O, buy, O buy the flowers!

if you can fancy any such to be uttered. The pot of fuchsias might be tendered to a passing customer; but it might equally well be upheld, without any ulterior object, for the mere sake of calling attention to its beauty. In fact, the predominant expression on the face of the pretty florist betokens a gentle sadness, that piques one's curiosity. Is it constitutional? **Or does** it tell the familiar tale **of** other days and happier **circumstances?** Physiognomists may decide; for a likeness is before them. Leaving **that point** unsettled, we have only to notice furthermore that youth and maturity are somewhat strangely blended in a countenance, which, in this respect at least, may serve as the type of American maidenhood. Maidens here—it is superfluous to add—are not much addicted to reverie, and are not prone to spoiling their comely features with the stamp of premature **seriousness.**

THE INTERRUPTED WEDDING.

G. FLUGGEN.

IN THE COLLECTION OF WILLIAM H. WEBB, ESQ.

THE slip between cup and lip, that forms the subject-matter of this composition, may perhaps be nearly as old as the institution of wedlock itself; it has certainly been done to death, in all varieties of shapes by playwrights and poetasters, especially since Walter Scott gave it fresh vogue by the power and pathos of his "Bride of Lammermuir." Nevertheless, it may be observed in passing, that this fine romance is best known to the public of to-day through the medium of Italian *prime donne*, who must needs, one after another, approach and woo every audience that is new to them, letting down their hair and exalting their voices, as desolate and maddened Lucias.

And, for the most part, the ballad-mongers and dramatists, and authors of startling tales for periodicals, show you a young lover rushing in upon the scene at the eleventh hour, to snatch the fair one, at the foot of the altar, from sacrifice to an expectant grey-beard. Not so, here. The personage assailed is a "braw wooer," of spruce attire and self-possessed presence; and Fate overtakes him—not in a rival for his lady-love's hand, but in a possible disputant for his own. Yet appearances do not indicate that this was a case of impending bigamy. The letters and the miniature tossed upon the floor, coupled with the deprecatory air of the venerable male intruder, who leads a downcast daughter or *protégée* by the hand, speak rather of an appeal to feeling, than of a threatened legal claim. The bridegroom wears the aspect of a thorough-paced man of the world, annoyed but not ashamed at this inauspicious advent. The bride and her relatives and friends, stamped also with the same air of worldliness, seem to be above all things indignant at the impudence of the interruption, taking it for granted that the abandonment of an early love is an affair of trivial moment.

Mr. Fluggen is of the school of Munich; and works of this class, delineating and satirizing evils, that are supposed to be inseparable from wealth, have become not unfrequent in German studios. It may be that the young artists of that land believe that the gentle sentiment, the domestic, the loving, has been exhausted by their predecessors, and that this impulsive age craves artistic food at once more novel and more stimulating. It may be that this is but a sign of seething political discontent. Be the cause what it may, social subjects are now often found on the Teutonic easel, and are too often treated in a bitter spirit. We hope that Society and Art may derive much mutual benefit from the contact; but we incline to doubt it.

THE VILLAGE POST-BOY.

EASTMAN JOHNSON.

IN THE GALLERY OF MARSHALL O. ROBERTS, ESQ.

UNLIKE nearly all his Dutch, and most of his German predecessors and contemporaries, and unlike his English brethren of to-day, known as Pre-Raphaelites, this American artist does not, in his excellent *genre* works, magnify his accessories into undue importance. They are **kept subordinate** to his main purpose, though made useful **enough** in their way. **Now they localize a** scene; now bring in a desirable bit of colour; **now help to give form to a** composition—still keeping **their place, and** taking nothing **off from the sentiment that rules.**

The two figures in this simple but attractive picture are well worth studying. The mail has arrived. Going his rounds, or bound to start upon them, the young post-man lingers over the cooking-stove, loth to face the biting air without. Brimful of importance, but very cold, and lazy perchance besides, he crouches over the kindly fire, having flung his letters on the ground, that he may devote himself to it without impediment. Conscious he may be of his great mission; but he is intent on warmth. As for the news —let it wait.

> Yet careless what he brings; his own concern
> Is to conduct it to the destined inn,
> And, having dropped the expected bag—pass on.
> To him indifferent whether grief or joy;
> Houses in ashes, and the fall of stocks;
> Births, **deaths, and marriages.**

Carlyle says that every boy, at a certain age, ought to be put under a barrel; and this bundle of self-esteem—who toasts his toes, instead of hurrying forward with his budget—may be at the very period of life indicated by the sarcastic philosopher. It is clear that he has passed the noisy and mischievous epoch, during which it must be a **chilled heart that cannot** sympathize with boyhood, and is beginning to take **his place** in the world, and to be vain moreover, of the fact. How oblivious is he of the presence of the shock-headed urchin in the chimney corner, though the latter, to our mind, is the more pleasant object of the two! This little fellow, with his round baby head and unkempt hair and chubby fist, sits silent meanwhile in his low arm-chair, biting his thumb, and regarding with meditative **and respectful attention his majestic hero** of the letter-bag. Perhaps he wonders **if the time will ever come, when he too** may attain the dignity of **wearing a** fur collar and mittens, and **be defiant of storms** and snow-drifts.

v

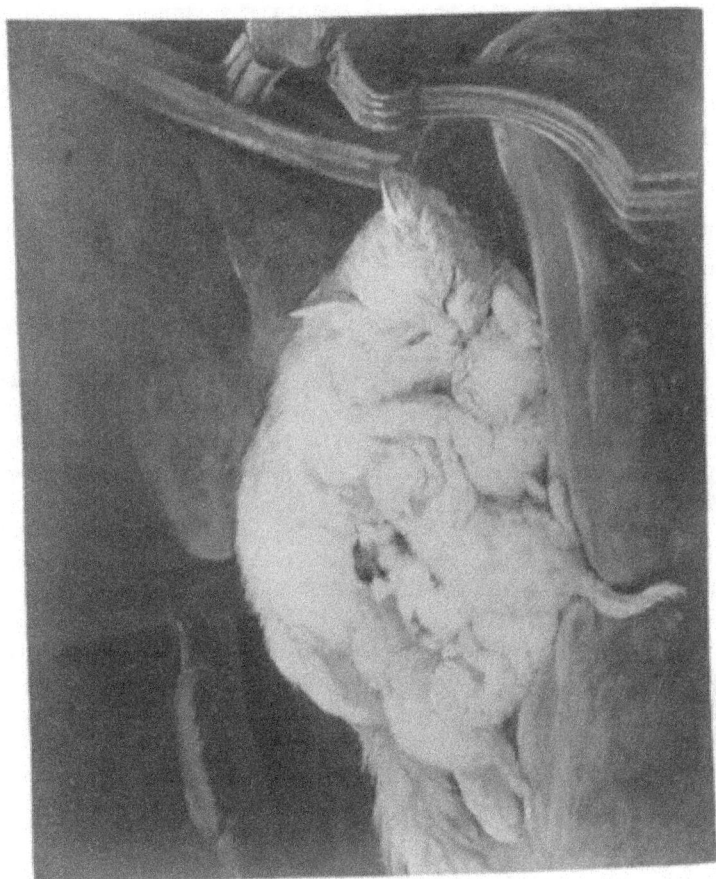

MATERNAL AFFECTION

MADAME PEYROL BONHEUR.

IN THE COLLECTION OF WILLIAM T. BLOODGETT ESQ

WITH profoundest **admiration for the** genius **and skill of** Mademoiselle **Rosa Bonheur**—who marshals ponderous Norman horses in long procession upon her canvas, **and** toys at ease with the most savage breed of Highland cattle—we must be permitted to doubt whether she could have treated such a subject as this, with **the tenderness and loving grace** thrown into it by her less famous sister. And this, **for the simple reason** that the former holds to her independence as Mademoiselle, while **the latter has** exchanged the maidenly for the married state, and may re-echo **that axiom—more** incontestably established than any other in human relations—"only **a mother can understand a mother's feelings."** If **any male reader has misgivings on this point, he is advised to express them to any lady of his acquaintance who chances to be "a joyful mother of children."**

The cat, it must be owned, has few friends. Presumed to be the confidential associate of witches, and known as a nocturnal brawler addicted to making night hideous, unsociable in disposition and hypocritical in demeanour, she is no favorite in life, and poets indite no flattering epitaphs, to be inscribed over her tomb—if she have one. Yet surely, when you watch her thus **ministering to the** wants of **sightless and** helpless infancy, thus enraptured in the exercise of her **fond** maternal instincts, it is impossible not to be touched. You tolerate, perhaps even patronize, the kitten, droll in its gambols, and merry playmate of girlhood and boyhood—why frown upon the unoffending creature, who, you perceive on the opposite page, is tremblingly alive to the pleasures of her calling, and without whom kittens would **not be ?**

> The heart is hard in nature, **and unfit**
> For human fellowship—as **being void**
> Of sympathy, and therefore dead alike
> To love and friendship both—that is not pleased
> With sight of animals enjoying life,
> Nor feels their happiness augment its own.

It were to be wished that the sun had given, in the **Photograph, a little more force to the lineaments of this fumbling and** blinking progeny, though **Madame Peyrol Bonheur is too** good an artist, to have endowed them with the marked features and pronounced expression of Grimalkin or Puss in Boots. As it is, the careful observer will not fail to note, that there may be much significance in very faint outlines.

It is grateful to add that this picture was painted and sold for the benefit of a charitable institution in Paris, the lady **having ceased to make professional use of her fine** talents, and employing them **only, thus and from time to time, in the cause of suffering humanity.**

VI

THE MISER ALARMED.

A. M. GUILLEMIN.

IN THE GALLERY OF AUGUST BELMONT, ESQ.

PAINTERS, and poets, and novelists—to say nothing of actual experience, and of the "eternal fitness of things"—have so long accustomed us to associate old age with the miserly life and habit, that we cannot call to mind any conspicuous instance, in which pen or pencil has dissevered the twain. A modern rhymester, it is true, did once ask, in a very general **way**:

> Oh! can it be good that a man should crave
> The dross of the world—so nigh his grave?

But the converse idea was not followed out, as it might have been for variety's sake. The veteran, of every one's acquaintance, reappeared, and was frightened out of his wits, or, rather, out of his enjoyment—as usual.

> He seeks the bed where he cannot rest;
> Made close beside his idol chest.
> He wakes with a wildered, haggard stare,
> For he dreams a thief is busy there.
> He searches around—the bolts are fast;
> And the watchmen of the night go past.
> His coffers are safe; but there's fear in his brain,
> And the miser cannot sleep again.

This is not a precise description of the hateful old fellow over **against** it; for he, notwithstanding his frowzy night-cap, shows no sign **of having sought his bed.** Neither, **in the accessories, is the wretch's stingy self-denial pushed to extremes**, after the manner of those over-scrupulous artists who are fearful lest their meaning should be missed, and so pile up explanatory adjuncts. If the water-jug indicates that our uneasy friend does not cloud his mind with generous potations, he can loll at least in a handsome and comfortable chair.

The pictorial merit of the figure speaks for itself; and it lends itself most kindly to the process of reproduction. Beyond this, it is not easy to eke out any remark from a theme that is worn so threadbare.

M. Guillemin is a Frenchman, and a distinguished painter of *genre* subjects.

EGYPTIAN CONSCRIPTS

J. L. GÉRÔME.

IN THE GALLERY OF **MARSHALL** O. ROBERTS, ESQ.

If this popular artist be given to what may be termed in common parlance "strong sensations," as in his famous "Duel after the Masked Ball" and his "Gladiators in the Amphitheatre Saluting Cæsar," he has the will and the ability to treat them in a grandiose manner. The sensational subject becomes, as it were, elevated by his genius. Thus the above title calls up the sad atrocity of those slave hunts in far away regions toward the apocryphal Mountains of the Moon, by means of which the armies of the Pachalic are often recruited; or it may remind one of the unsparing and ruthless administration within the better known Valley of the Nile, where spade or musket must perforce be wielded at the bidding of a despotic taskmaster. Substitutes and commutation-taxes are not recognized as part of the system there. The Pacha wants labourers—they are summoned; soldiers—they are enrolled. Add, to such ideas as these, the filth and degradation undeniably prevalent among the modern tribes of Egypt, and you might look at best for a disagreeable picture.

On the contrary, the original has nothing repulsive in it, save in one respect. The yoke, by which the two foremost couples of Conscripts are secured together, alone intimates directly that they are not Volunteers. Otherwise, their portly figures, their majestic tread, the fact that they are not nude but costumed after the picturesque fashion of the East, and the unembarrassed bearing of their conductor, might lead to a different inference. Gérôme has undertaken to illustrate a painful scene; but he has dealt with it, one might almost say, poetically.

For, was not this absence of all accessories purposely designed? Behind these victims of an odious raid may be, in imagination, their homes in Darfour or Sennaar; before them the abhorred discipline of Cairo or Damietta. But immediately around them is spread out the sand of the Desert—and that alone; only foot-prints in the foreground show that others have trodden the same melancholy route; the hot mist veils the numbers of the actual company. In dispensing then with painful adjuncts, as also with the accustomed palm tree, or distant minaret, or glimpse of the Nile, or "bit" from Thebes or Philæ, it can hardly be doubted that the painter had his own intent. Without dwelling thereupon, and without entering upon the fertile theme of subjective and objective styles —as wide apart in Art as in Literature—it may be added that what is, and what is not, on this particular canvas, work together to the highest end; it is at once suggestive and impressive.

THE REAPER'S REST.

W. SHAYER.

IN POSSESSION OF JOHN C. FORCE, ESQ.

This English artist, who is probably more appreciated and admired in this country than in his own, adheres with fond pertinacity to subjects drawn from rural life. His wandering down to the sea-shore—exemplified on another page of this volume—is but a variation from the rule; the characteristics are the same, the accessories only being changed. Professedly, not a landscape nor a *genre* painter, in the ordinary acceptation of either term, he blends together some of the attractions of both, after a fashion peculiarly his own. He does not idealize or experiment upon the forms, the tints, the atmospheric effects, the struggles of the elements, or any of the profounder mysteries of Nature; he does not affect to make his easel give lessons in social science. Yet his trees are faithfully copied from originals in the New Forest of Hampshire, in the neighbourhood of which is his modest residence; and their nicely-delineated foliage often looks down upon groups of humble figures, transcribed from actual observation, while suiting admirably his general design.

In two points, Mr. Shayer's rustic figures differ from not a few of their rivals on canvas. One is this: drawn from living likenesses among the lowly and the labouring classes, they can never be mistaken for ladies and gentlemen masquerading. Their other distinction—and a very grateful one it is—consists herein: they never convey that sense of degradation and misery, which some artists, and very many writers, invariably associate with the "simple annals of the poor."

As for the scene and the persons on the opposite page, what travelled or well-read American does not recognize it and them at once? They are so thoroughly English, that there is no mistaking them. It may be noted, however, that such memorials as this of contemporary rural England are likely to become scarce, inasmuch as the face of the land and the habits of the people, in the farming districts, are undergoing a rapid change. Utilitarianism is fatally busy—fatally, that is, to the artist. Systematic and economic principles are pulling down many a thatched and quaintly-gabled cottage, that sheltered "the forefathers of the hamlet," and are substituting more useful but very ugly buildings of brick and slate. Machinery, no less than chemistry, is extensively applied to agriculture. Harvests will soon be all garnered by steam. Then will it be true—though in a different sense from that in which Mrs. Hemans wrote it—that "the reaper's task is done."

THE CABARET.

JULES BRÉTON.

IN POSSESSION OF JOHN HOEY, ESQ.

THE Sun, under the popular process of the day, is as close a copyist as a Chinaman. Because varnish had been applied to Jules Bréton's canvas, before the pigments were thoroughly dry, and numerous cracks had in consequence made themselves obtrusively visible on the surface, the Sun must needs make this fact patent, and thus mar in some degree an otherwise fair transcript of a singularly powerful work.

Powerful; but not pleasant. This inside view of humble life in a Normandy wine-shop makes no appeal to one's social or personal sympathies, and must be admired solely for its eminent artistic worth. Neither has the sentiment,—such as it is—that pervades the scene, any local or special mark. It is not in French villages alone, that indignant wives of the peasant class summon home from groggeries unwilling husbands; nor there only, that labour expends its hard gains in pernicious resorts.

At the same time it may be observed, that there is nothing absolutely repulsive in the subject or its treatment. A dash even of the humorous, if not of the pathetic, is to be detected in the central group. The inanity, the tipsy bewilderment, the meanness of expression, the personal fear—the entire moral degradation, that characterises the village pettifogger surprised in his cups, and shrinking from his wife's vigorous arm, contrasts notably with the threatening attitude and earnest action of the woman herself. Is it too much moreover, to fancy, in the dog's mute appeal to his master, a fellow-feeling of the danger that may ensue, if the mistress's order be not obeyed?

The figures, indeed, ought to be studied together, and separately. Rare skill is exhibited in the combination, no less than in the individuality. The old Garde Champêtre, drowsing over his cards, is French to the backbone; you may almost hear him snore. With what readiness, too, as though accustomed to such reproaches, the serving-woman behind him replies to the imbecile fellow in the white nightcap, who is evidently complaining of the quantity or the quality of his potation! What thorough rustics, also, are the sporting couple, on the opposite side! The female irruption is to them a casual pastime; you are sure that they have been poaching a score of times, under the nose of the sleepy gamekeeper. The whole, and the parts, we repeat, should be carefully studied.

x

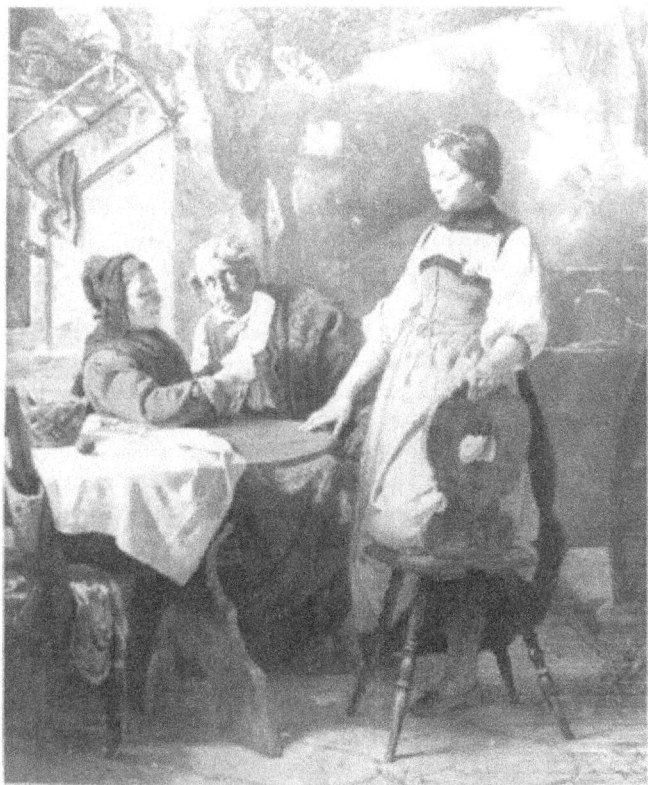

THE PROPOSAL.

B. VAUTIER.

IN THE GALLERY OF MARSHALL O. ROBERTS, ESQ.

In the absence of any direct record of the artist's purpose, this title would seem to be appropriate for a composition, whose charm consists in its pervading air of simplicity and truth. The expression of astonishment and doubt on the face of the listening father might suggest an interrupted love-letter—subject common enough, by the way, with limner as with novelist; but this may be otherwise explained.

Given up to their own pursuits, men of mature age—fathers even—are for the most part lacking in sympathy with the affections of the young; whereas woman—no matter what her years—rarely fails to feel a woman's interest in affairs of the heart, irrespective of the claims of relationship. Thus it is not German, and not humble life alone, that is here typified by the artist; he appeals to the wide range of human experience. Natural, under the circumstances, is the half wondering, half suspicious look of the old man, who has long ago forgotten that ever he was young himself; and well does it contrast with the gratified air of the matron, whom one might almost imagine carried back, on the other hand, to the days of her own golden prime, while rejoicing for and with her child. As Burns has it, in "The Cotter's Saturday Night:"

> Well pleased the mother hears it's nae wild, worthless rake.

Accustomed as one is too often, in this polished age, to have loving woman served up both by pen and pencil, in an atmosphere of meretricious grace, this earnest, trusting, modest German maiden is a grateful study of the sex, despite her homeliness and inelegant attitude. The plain truth is, this "Proposal" touches a universal chord of sympathy, and hence is a universal favourite.

H

WILLIAM THE SILENT WOMANLY DEVOTION

PENNEMAN.

IN THE GALLERY OF AUGUST BELMONT, ESQ

You suppose this—and not unnaturally—to be a **dying scene; but the illustrious** sufferer, stricken nigh to death and with his head supported on **so fair a pillow, did not** on this occasion succumb to the assassin. It may scarcely be doubted **that he owed the** prolongation of his life, in some degree at least, to the assiduous **and tender nursing of** his wife. During eighteen days and nights, with briefest intervals of repose, she sat by the bed-side of her husband, ministering to his relief and comfort, in the manner here depicted. His physical pain and overwhelming anxiety for the State were only alleviated, while she was at his side.

The man who was the object of this touching fidelity, this infinite love, was the famous Prince of Orange, known by the title inscribed above. The woman was Charlotte de Bourbon, his third wife, daughter of the Duc de Montpensier, who was one of the most prominent Catholic Princes of France. The lady herself had been forced in early youth to enter a Convent, and had indeed become its Abbess; but, when the champion of the Reformation wooed and won her, she was a refugee **at the Court of the Elector** Palatine, having renounced the faith of her family and **become a convert to Protestantism.**

She had been married not quite seven years, and had **borne to William of Nassau six** daughters, when, in March, 1582, his life was **attempted at Antwerp.** Desperately wounded by a pistol-shot, the Prince lay for some time in a most critical condition, yet not altogether without amendment and hope of recovery. On the eighteenth day, however, so dangerous a hæmorrhage supervened, that the end was thought to have come; and now, exhausted by long watchings and anxious care, the strength of the self-sacrificing Charlotte gave way. She was seized with **a violent fever, lingered a few weeks,** and finally died on the 5th of May—solemn thanksgivings for William's recovery having been offered up, only three days previously.

History, barren for the most part in gentle episodes, records few such beautiful and affecting incidents. It is proper to add that the Prince of Orange had been a fond and faithful husband to this, his **third wife. But it may not be omitted, that he** espoused his fourth and last—a **widowed daughter of the great Admiral de Coligny—in less than** twelve months after **the third had laid down her life in the effort to preserve his!**

This picture is by **the Court painter of the present King of Holland.**

A PORTRAIT FROM THE LIFE.

J. CARPENDALE.

JULES GÉRARD, or Gordon Cumming, or some other mighty Nimrod, tells of an occasion on which he and a huge lion found themselves looking steadily into each other's eyes, with a low bush only intervening between them. It can scarcely be doubted, that the animal held the man to be the queerest beast that ever fell in his way.

But suppose for a moment, that the huntsman—in place of quietly adjusting to his shoulder his double-barrelled Devismes or Manton—had **simply** brought his vis-à-vis within range of a Daguerrean apparatus, and that the result of **such scientific** encounter had been **the Photograph on the opposite page.** What would be the **inference?** Surely, if the countenance may be read, it must be that the lion looked upon his strange visitor with the most ineffable contempt. Surprise at the intrusion, and a little latent anger, may perhaps also be detected, yet subordinate to his sovereign disdain.

Now, it need hardly be said, that this supposition is not based on truth. Every one knows that the Cumming and the Gérard cared more for a dead carcase, than for a living likeness. It was not therefore in Libyan desert or in Caffrarian jungle, that this grand specimen of his race sat or stood for **his portrait;** nor was **his** portrait taken, in the first instance, by the process to which **allusion has been made.** Neither, on the other hand, is this an offspring of the **artist's imagination—a Leo the** Magnificent, or a Lion of the Tribe of Judah—as might **be surmised** from **its noble** mien and majesty of deportment. The original is actually in possession of **Mr.** Wallack, though that popular gentleman maintains no such four-footed **pet for his private** delectation, **and** thrusts none such upon his stage, **in the part usually played by Snug the** Joiner, when "**A Midsummer Night's Dream" is given, lest his roar should "fright** the ladies." Mr. Carpendale did indeed copy from the life, standing face to face with the lordly brute here represented. **But the interview** between the pair took place in this good **city of New York, and there was** something stouter between them than a tuft of gorse. Whether **this** was under canvas or within brick walls, in museum or menagerie, **is** altogether unimportant. It is mainly obvious, from his proud and scornful look, **that** the animal in question was imbued, to some extent, with the philosophy of Lovelace, who sang that

Stone walls do not **a prison make,**
Nor iron bars a cage.

The original, it may be added, is not an oil-painting, but an extremely clever drawing in coloured crayons.

XIII

JORDANS.

IN POSSESSION OF HENRY L. JAQUES, ESQ.

INEXHAUSTIBLE is the variety of modes, in which the German tendency to what the world calls "sentiment" is displayed; but seldom is it shown on canvas with more touching simplicity and effect, than in the original, whereof the counterpart is before you. The subject is not profound, nor is it treated with any excess of elaboration; rather it is so nicely balanced, that it were hard to say whether the ideal or the material predominates—the point being open, as it usually is, to the sympathetic taste of the spectator.

One admirer, therefore, will deduce, from this little episode in domestic life, a whole store of speculations as to the past of the good couple before him, and as to the mutual relations existing between them. Another will mainly note the precision of the drawing and the "naturalness" of its details—how heavily the worthy dame is sleeping, and how delicately her husband is reminding her that his reading has not come to an end. And both the realist and the idealist will be in the right of it. Painting is, or should be, simultaneously imitative and suggestive; and they lose half the pleasure that Art confers, who can but view it in one light alone.

Illustrators of Burns's Poems, who have taken in hand "John Anderson, my Jo!", always intensify their moral by accessories that betoken poverty; being, like many around them, set in the belief that the phrase, "poor but honest," is laudatory in a double sense. Jordans, on the contrary—doing justice to human nature, and warranted by countless examples in his own land—chooses to depict a prosperous looking old man engaged in entertaining or instructing his portly spouse, and rousing her only by the gentlest of touches, when his sense of propriety, and, perhaps, his personal vanity, have both sustained a wound. We must confess that this forbearance and this delicacy are enhanced, in our mind, rather than diminished, by the absence of any attempt at sensational contrast. So, too, with the good frau. She is daintily clad; yet her flesh is weak. She has been "sent to sleep with sound"; but there is no sign that she is "waked with silence." Yet best is it, oh slumberer, as it is! Sleep on! You have been caught at a happy moment by the artist. Your waking hours could not have inspired him better. Under no circumstances could he have portrayed, more deftly and more acceptably, that model husband, whose love and patience stand the test of a drowsy listener.

THE FAIR HOUSEKEEPER.

DAVID DE NOTER.

IN THE GALLERY OF MARSHALL O. ROBERTS, ESQ.

A FELICITOUS illustration this of the prosaic side of "Love's young dream"! The young wife, her own housekeeper, is in her store-room, taking inventory of the articles supplied for family consumption, or planning, perhaps, on behalf of her husband's guests,

> on hospitable thoughts intent,
> What choice to choose for delicacy best.

Arrayed in simple attire, as becoming to her youthful style of beauty and appropriate to her domestic avocation, you still smile to read upon the lady's countenance her sense of exceeding responsibility. Surely, she must have been but a short time married, and is over-anxious therefore as to the importance of the duties she has assumed. Her person indeed indicates that the rosebud has not yet ripened into the perfect flower, though, from her grave aspect in the assumption of household cares, it is clear that she will soon be numbered among those blooming dames of whom the poet has said:

> With beauties so maturely fair,
> Affecting, mild, and manifold,
> Can girlish charms no more compare
> Than nect'rines green with nect'rines gold.

Had he, the poet, we wonder, been feasting his eyes upon certain of these Flemish gems of art, that make the mouth water in more senses than one, when he hit upon this not very flattering similitude? Possibly, for the accessories in them may not often be overlooked, even if it were not true, in some instances, that they constitute the principal objects, whereto the human figure becomes subordinate.

But no such indignity has here been offered by David De Noter to humanity, or to the sex. The lady queens it over her surroundings, while leaving them to speak up well for themselves. Thus, you can decide that the time is late summer or early autumn—by the open door through which the sunshine finds it way, by the game-birds hanging on the wall, by certain of the vegetables strewed upon the floor. This provision, which includes a lobster—but does not include the grosser viands, lest temptation be thrown in the demure cat's way—announces a savory "banquet toward." At the board, you are well assured that no presence will be more gracious or more graceful, than that of the Fair Housekeeper herself.

WILLIAM OF ORANGE.

G. TERBURG.

IN THE GALLERY OF THOMAS J. BRYAN, ESQ.

It is presumed by the owner, but is not established beyond possibility of doubt, that this curious portrait represents the youthful Prince, subsequently known as William the Third, of England. It is on record that the artist did paint such an one at the urgent request of the Prince, whose cause in the Netherlands he had warmly espoused; and that it is the work of Terburg's own hand is attested alike by internal evidence, and by his signature, which the learned in these matters pronounce undeniably authentic.

The characteristics of William's earlier years—noted by his contemporaries, and expounded by more modern writers—speak visibly in the personage before you. Look to it well; mark the head; study the countenance; observe even the pose and bearing. Then read one expression, borrowed from Macaulay's History of England, and you will surely conclude that the written and the painted portraitures singularly accord. At the opening of one of his chapters, he drops the terse but comprehensive remark, in reference to the Prince of Orange—"indeed, it might be said that he had never been young." The historian presently amplifies the idea, though still with the conciseness and vigour that belonged to him. We can make room for one other only of his remarks: "Since Octavius, the world has seen no such instance of precocious statesmanship."

In the shrewdness, and gravity, and self-possession, and wariness of this face, may not something of the youth's strange gifts, something of the man's great destiny, be read?

In the original, the doublet and hose and sash being all orange-coloured, and the long-flowing hair being of yellowish-auburn, the effect is unique and striking. The picture, in fact, would be perfect in its kind, but for the multiplicity and inferior treatment of the accessories. These are so huddled together, and so manifestly detract from the power and dignity of the figure, that we cannot avoid suspecting them to be the work of an inferior artist, superadded at some subsequent period in the fulness of flattery and of bungling. Was it needful that a serpent should protrude his ungainly head, to let the world know that William of Orange was wise beyond his fellows? Must the greyhound tell that he was vigilant; the spaniel that he was faithful; the snail that he was patient; the watch that he was punctual; the skull, the truncheon of command, the helmet, the shell—all vouch emblematically for his manifold virtues? By no means. Terburg was a portrait-painter; he would not have thus overloaded and spoiled his subject. He was a *genre* painter; if he had himself introduced these typical odds-and-ends, at least he would have rendered them better.

THE WALK ON THE TABLE.

F. E. MEÏERHEIM.

IN THE COLLECTION OF WILLIAM H. WEBB, ESQ.

In casting about for a suitable title, whereby to designate this clear transcript of a pleasant original, "The First Walk" naturally suggests itself. That infantile first walk is an event of such supreme importance in the household, such an era in the little life of the little subject! But, with due remembrance that precocity, mental or physical, is not the order of the day among the Teutons, it is hard to believe that this is the very commencement of going alone. So tall a young lassie must have essayed already the sanded floor or the softer grass-plot; not to dwell on the improbability that so ticklish a *début* would be ventured amid the extra perils of cups and saucers. There remains therefore the theory, that this is the earliest occasion, on which the well-grown baby has been permitted thus to diversify the pleasures of the table, for the entertainment of a happy family.

And not Blondin himself, accomplishing one of his most dangerous walks upon the ever-threatening cord of Fate, can have experienced such sense of gleeful triumph as fills the bosom of the adventurous maiden here practising her steps.

> No heart gives such ecstatic thumps
> In spur-decked boots or perfumed pumps;
> *   *   *   *   *   *
> Most truly then my tiny toes
> Walked in a path *couleur de rose*.

As for comparison between the feelings of an idle crowd, that scarcely knows whether it hopes most, or fears most, that a fall from the exhibitor's break-neck height may titillate them with a new sensation—as for comparison between their gaping wonder, and the thrill of pure but tremulous delight that possesses the mother watching her child's early essay such as this, it were absolutely odious to attempt it.

A peculiarity, that must become more and more rare in pictures of European everyday life, remains to be mentioned in reference to this grateful composition. As international communications are multiplied, and manufactured fabrics for common wear are scattered far and wide by commercial enterprise, local costume is disappearing. Quaint and picturesque distinctions will soon be no more. The learned in such matters will soon be puzzled to know, by his garb, whether the peasant hail from Rhineland or the Tyrol.

E. VERBOECKHOVEN.

IN THE GALLERY OF WILLIAM P. WRIGHT, ESQ.

Nor more famous among agriculturists in his day was "Old Coke, of Norfolk," for improving the breed of sheep, than is this Belgian artist for his fidelity in transferring them to canvas. But a motive for the gentleman farmer's ambition and painstaking is obvious. It was a grand bucolic feat, to raise at once the quality of wool and of mutton. It is not so easy to account for Verboeckhoven's choice. Did he aspire to rivalry with Cuyp's cows, or Wouverman's infallible grey horse? The whole animal race was at his disposition; and how well he wrought upon one attractive and manifold species of it is evident on an early page of this volume. Sheep, indeed, in groups or in masses, dotting green hill-sides, or folded by the shepherd's care, may become valuable accessories of landscape. As individuals, very masterly handling can alone make their portraiture acceptable—and in achieving this result there must be a perpetual struggle against the want of colours grateful to the eye, and the lack of either grace or expression in form. Among domesticated beasts, on the contrary—with the dog pointing his game, the horse rising at a leap, even the cat crouching ere she springs upon a mouse—how the outline varies with the action, how unerringly it speaks of the intent!

And as though to mark still more strongly its ingrained homeliness, the ewe in question gives us her face in profile. Certes, there is no line of beauty here; and so your eye involuntarily drops down upon the pretty group at her feet. Are they not charming, these little kids, in their perfect simplicity? How knowing is the look of the more prominent one in white! How he seems to be musing on past gambols, or projecting future romps! How well is the latent fun of his baby countenance contrasted with the solemn gravity of his mother's! In one and all, what tokens of nice touch and fidelity to living models!

Again; the apparent silence and repose might have been deemed monotonous, had not relief been skilfully provided by the bustling ducks in the foreground. As their gay plumage enlivens the somewhat sombre tints that prevail, so does their movement give animation to an otherwise slumbrous scene. Amphibious and restless and most adventurous birds; truly, ye are a type of the old Norsemen or the modern Anglo-Saxons! We often think of you as so many Captain Cooks, when we see you exploring round and round your appointed world. Has not the circular pond, so familiar to us, for you its inexhaustible store of Otaheites and Owhyhees?

XVIII

THE COUNCIL OF BLOOD.

LOUIS GALLAIT.

IN THE GALLERY OF AUGUST BELMONT, ESQ.

The reign of terror instituted in the Netherlands by the Duke of Alva, as representative of Philip II, was made up of a series of incidents so awful, that the mind even now sickens at its story plainly told. In sanguinary subjects it is more prolific than the martyrdoms of all the Saints on record.

Elsewhere, in this collection, it is seen how **Gallait drew from this source,** and how successfully he grappled with a scene that a less masterly hand would have **vulgarized.** Here is no trunkless **head, no corpse, no victim.** Yet does the **picture possess the impressionable spectator with a terrible fascination.** Conceived in a grandiose spirit, and wrought up to perfection with consummate skill—as is obvious in the transcript here offered—it is marked by one peculiarity, which the transcript refuses to convey. The conceit may be imaginary on our part; but it seems to us, in looking at the original, as though the very atmosphere were suffused with blood. No one, standing before it, can fail to realize that it is charged to the full with the magnetism of power; nor do we hesitate to pronounce it the finest historical painting in this country.

In the eloquent pages of Motley's "Rise of the Dutch Republic," the famous Blood Council is described as an informal contrivance for facilitating wholesale executions. Of Vargas, one of Alva's "two Spanish blood-hounds," here represented as going through the superfluous formula of an oath, on taking upon him the office of its President, it is said : "He executed Alva's bloody work with an industry which was almost superhuman, and with a merriment which would have shamed **a demon.** His execrable jests ring through the **blood and smoke and death-cries of those days of** perpetual sacrifice." Of Alva himself, the historian remarks with comprehensive conciseness: "He did not combine a great variety of vices, but those which he had were colossal; and he possessed no virtues. He was neither lustful nor intemperate; but his professed eulogists admitted his enormous avarice, while the world has agreed that such an amount of stealth and ferocity, of patient vindictiveness and universal bloodthirstiness, was never found in a savage beast of the forest, and but rarely in a human bosom."

Of these five powerful but most forbidding countenances, each of which is a study, the Priest's alone, who uplifts the Cross, offers any redeeming quality. There is something in religious zeal that ennobles, even though it work through bad means to a bad end.

XIX

THE SCARLET LETTER.

E. LEUTZE.

IN THE COLLECTION OF ABRAHAM M. COZZENS, ESQ.

THESE portraitures of Hester Prynne and Little Pearl—albeit imaginary likenesses of ideal persons—will be hailed as life-like, by all who are familiar with Hawthorne's rueful and awful romance; gratefully so perhaps by those of them, who, being profoundly impressed by the author's written characterization, are yet unable to shape it vividly before their mind's eye. And this the more, inasmuch as the artist has delineated with most subtle power the hapless mother and the weird child of the book.

It would be inappropriate to condense here, in a few lines, for the benefit of those who never read it, the strange tale so forcibly told. It is enough to say that the woman before you could but dwell upon an agonizing past, a tumultuous present, and a dreary and doubtful future. For the rest, let us cite the little that is needed in the way of description.

Of Hester Prynne, says Hawthorne, in allusion to the period indicated by her young companion's age: "All the light and graceful foliage of her character had been withered up. * * Even the attractiveness of her person had undergone a similar change. * * There seemed to be no longer anything in Hester's face for Love to dwell upon; nothing in Hester's form, though majestic and statue-like, that Passion would ever dream of clasping in its embrace; nothing in Hester's bosom to make it ever again the pillow of Affection. * * Much of the marble coldness of Hester's impression was to be attributed to the circumstance that her life had turned, in a great measure, from passion and feeling, to thought." Has not much, very much, of all this been caught and embodied by the Painter?

So also with Pearl, little Pearl. Thus it is written of her, in scattered passages: "The child's own nature had something wrong in it, which continually betokened that she had been born amiss—the effluence of her mother's lawless passion. * * Hester was ultimately compelled to stand aside, and permit the child to be swayed by her own impulses. * * She could recognize her wild, desperate, defiant mood, the flightiness of her temper, and even some of the very cloud-shapes of gloom and despondency that had brooded in her heart. * * And see with what natural skill she has made those simple flowers adorn her! Had she gathered pearls and diamonds and rubies, in the wood, they could not have become her better!" Is not the wild and wayward and outgoing expression of the elfin-child as well conveyed, as the deeply introspective look of Hester Prynne?

II

THE BONE OF CONTENTION.

ALFRED DE DREUX.

IN POSSESSION OF JOHN HOEY ESQ

WHAT lounger at print-shop windows is not familiar **with Alfred de Dreux's horses?** Who does not recollect them caracolling with all four feet at once in the air, **and rivalling** the ponies of Sir Benjamin Backbite, inasmuch as

Their legs are so slim and their tails are so long?

Who can ever forget his dandies aping Paladins **of the Empire, his Amazonian Princesses—of the Circus?** Yet, if in his equestrian portraits and fancy pieces he treads the ticklish border between the sublime and the ridiculous, he is none the less in vogue along the Parisian Boulevard. He is, for all that, the Horace Vernet of the Bois de Boulogne.

But Alfred de Dreux's dogs may not be criticised in this fashion. In dealing with them, he limits himself to a study of animal nature, finding no special occasion to lend his brush to the display of human vanity. And here, accordingly, is an admirable specimen of his power—spirited, life-like, full of movement and expression, and imbued moreover with a strong dash of that latent humour which **is the charm** of some of Landseer's master-pieces.

A casual look at the trio might perhaps call to mind the old hit at the lawyers, wherein one of that cunning race is represented as encouraging a quarrel between clients, in order that he may secure a prize for himself. We do not, however, thus interpret the painter's meaning. We take it that the wide-awake gentleman, who throws himself into position up above, having already made an excellent dinner **off the bone that** lies in the foreground, **had retired for a comfortable snooze to an inviting bed of hay. Two strollers, with keener appetites, coming at the same moment upon the neglected remnant of his feast, are just commencing the prelude of snarl and growl that bodes a fight for the coveted morsel, and the noise awakes him from his nap. He starts up, all alive with the instincts of his pugnacious breed, and appears to be** intimating to **the intruders that they need not trouble** themselves in disposing of his property. "Ha! my fine fellows," you might almost imagine him to be saying, "leave that bone alone; it belongs to me—or else, take care of yourselves!"

The strong points in this clever composition are easily recognized. Among them may be noted the queer side-long glances of the prominent pair—so true to reality—as though each **had one eye upon the bone, and the other on his rival; the mutual anger** and jealousy, **well conveyed by arched tail and bristling hair; the bull-terrier's audacious and self-reliant air of supremacy.**

LAST HONOURS TO EGMONT AND HORN.

LOUIS GALLAIT.

IN THE GALLERY OF WILLIAM P. WRIGHT, ESQ.

History and tradition both record that after the execution of the Counts Egmont and Horn, at Brussels, on the 5th of June, 1568, and after two hours' exposure upon the scaffold, their lifeless remains were borne in stately procession through the streets, and were then laid out upon a bier beneath the high altar of St. Gudule.

But tradition and history are not agreed, in respect to the closing scene of the judicial murder then enacted. Gallait, adhering to the popular belief, depicts the heads of the illustrious sufferers exposed to view upon a fair white pillow. Certain contemporary writers, whose statement is adopted by Mr. Motley in his "History of the Dutch Republic," declare that they were immediately enclosed in boxes and despatched to Madrid, so that "the king was thus enabled to look upon the dead faces of his victims, without the trouble of a journey to the Provinces"! Gallait, it should be remembered, is a Belgian and a resident of Brussels; and, as he treats his lofty subjects grandly and earnestly, it is presumed that he had authority for his version.

Prominent among the gazers is a figure sometimes mistaken for the Duke of Alva himself, to whom he bears an extraordinary resemblance. But there is reason to believe that Gallait intended this for Ferdinand, the Duke's natural son, in whose forced attendance on this supreme occasion may be read another instance of the refinement of cruelty, which characterized the sanguinary monster. Ferdinand had in youth been captivated by the graceful bearing and winning qualities of Egmont. Ferdinand's father compelled him to aid in arresting the Count, as now to assist at these fearful obsequies.

It has been sometimes objected, that the subject of this eloquent work is too revolting for the legitimate purposes of art. The author of a slight but very able sketch of Count Egmont's career—published lately in London, and written especially with reference to the use that Goethe, Schiller, and Gallait have made of his story—says, with much force and truth: "The meaning of the picture is not to excite horror by depicting the gory heads of beheaded criminals. The men whose heads lie on that pillow, illumined by sickly light from the altar of Rome, were no criminals. * * It is their death, rather than them dead, that M. Gallait has depicted. There is no gloating over blood-stains, or the details which would pander to the vulgar appetite for the horrible. All the horror is lightly touched. * * There is a noble reticence and modesty in this part of the treatment." This, we repeat, is well and truly put.

The original, in Mr. Wright's Gallery, is of cabinet size, and is a copy made by the artist himself, from the large picture done by him for Tournay, his native city.

THE FRUIT-DEALER.

A. VAN HAMME.

IN THE GALLERY OF MARSHALL O. ROBERTS, ESQ.

GERARD DOUW, Metzu, Mieris, and others of **the famous** Dutch painters of their period, have been reproached, by later and captious critics, with a too slavish fidelity to the objects they represented. In truth, they **were not prone to** idealizing. **Their** Burgomasters' handsome **wives** and daughters **rarely figured as** Arcadian **shepherdesses.** The brilliant hues **of their tulips, on canvas, were transferred** direct **from their own gorgeous flower-beds.** **Vessels of gold and silver plate,** brightly polished **kitchen utensils, and the good things destined to fill them—all were** at hand and **were faithfully copied.**

Yet, in one respect, these literal interpreters sometimes took a liberty—and **with results** undeniably charming. They set their portraitures **of** local domestic **life** within a frame of their own invention. Not only did they group well, and pose **well,** gracious ladies of high degree amid luxurious accessories, and buxom wenches **amid** culinary furniture and garden products; they garnished the whole—kitchen or parlour, maid or mistress, all the details on which they lovingly laboured—with certain architectural and sculptured devices, right pleasant to the eye, if unknown in such juxta-position. An Italian, striving for the same effect, would have placed his figures under **a** ruined **archway; a** German, **beneath the portico of a church;** a Frenchman, in **an opera-box.** **The living Van Hamme, in this dainty composition, does but** follow his **admired predecessors, when he boldly deviates so far from the truth. You might search through all the streets of Leyden or the Hague, without finding the counterpart of this fantastic house. Could there be one, nevertheless, better fitted for setting off the** persons thus fantastically grouped ?

The brilliant colouring of the original is remarkable ; and, if that may not be given here, at least this Photograph is conspicuous for the clearness and delicacy with which the modelling and shading are reproduced.

AN ASSAULT AT CONSTANTINE.

HORACE VERNET.

IN THE GALLERY OF AUGUST BELMONT, ESQ.

This incident in the **French campaign of Algeria in 1837 deserves careful examina-tion, for it** exhibits **something more than the ordinary—or, rather, extraordinary—merits, that have placed Horace Vernet at the head of all modern painters of battle-pieces.**

Notwithstanding the paucity of figures introduced, it forms in itself a complete episode of war, a stirring and a striking one. In the handful of combatants—only a score or so in number—what variety is there of action and expression! How much is suggested! **How entirely** absent is that tendency to theatrical excess, **which** is **common to** works of this class, and from which even this grand artist is not always free! There is indeed a terrible earnestness in the assailants; yet it is not altogether unmixed with that instinctive clutching at shelter from a murderous fire, which the best and bravest of soldiers may manifest. One officer shields himself for the moment behind a project-ing abutment. The men, who carry on their shoulders the bags of powder used for blow-ing in doors or blowing up obstructions, lean towards the same precarious covering. On **the** other hand, Lamoricière, the hero of the scene and the **leader of this** forlorn **hope, stands out** conspicuous **in the** enfiladed **gateway,** and **presses forward the freshly gathering troops to the attack. He it was who, in the course of his brilliant services in Africa, organized the corps of Zouaves. He was their Colonel at the period represented.**

But this earnestness and this reality are not limited to the fighting element. Beside the dead are the wounded and the dying; and from their faces " the **light of battle**" has **evidently** passed for **ever.** Seldom is crushed humanity depicted with ghastlier or more piteous force. Without the aid of colour, even in this semblance of a fine sepia drawing, each head and each figure is in itself a study.

Horace Vernet executed this fine work in duplicate; but the duplicate, which belonged to Louis Philippe, was burned at the Palace of Neuilly, during the Revolution **of** 1848.

HETTY AND THE INDIANS.

SCHUSSEL.

A VERY graphic illustration this, of an incident recorded in the eleventh chapter of Cooper's "Deerslayer," the first of the celebrated "Leather Stocking Tales." The story extends over the period between 1740 and 1745. The locality is the wilderness of New York State, at that time but thinly settled. The Indians here are Hurons, who are out on "the war-path." They have made two prisoners—Henry March, a young hunter, commonly known as Hurry-Harry, from "a dashing, reckless, off-hand manner, and a physical restlessness that kept him constantly on the move"—and Thomas Hutter, commonly called Floating Tom, from the fact of his passing much time in a scow or "ark" upon one of the smaller lakes. These persons, the author tells us, had ventured on shore to bring off several canoes which they feared the savages would discover, and also, if possible—*horresco referens*—to scalp any of those gentry whom they might meet. But they failed in their object, and caught a Tartar.

Thus it chanced that the "ark," and Hutter's two daughters, Judith and Hetty by name, were left to the care of the Deerslayer. Hetty, the younger, we are told, was extremely pious and somewhat feeble-minded. Moved by filial love and by the religious promptings of her unreasoning mind, this poor girl determines to go on shore to the Indian encampment, and endeavour by intercession and reading of the Scriptures to save her father's life. A little tender feeling toward his companion is moreover hinted.

Having escaped from the "ark" and the protection of Deerslayer, she fulfils this design; and here the scene is represented. The artist has followed Cooper's description very closely. It commences thus : " As Hetty approached the Chiefs, they opened their little circle with an ease and deference of manner that would have done credit to men of more courtly origin. A fallen tree lay near, and the oldest of the warriors made a quiet sign for the girl to be seated on it, taking his place at her side, with all the gentleness of a father. The others arranged themselves around the two with grave dignity ; and then the girl, who had sufficient observation to perceive that such a course was expected of her, began to reveal the object of her visit." * * " She reverently unrolled a small English Bible from its envelope of coarse calico ; treating the volume with the sort of external respect that a Romanist would be apt to show to a religious relic."

As to the results of the poor girl's mission—it surprises no reader to find that she is unsuccessful.

BEFORE THE WIND.

T. S. ROBINS.

IN POSSESSION OF WILLIAM YOUNG, ESQ.

Rude and ungainly as they may be, the fishing craft of the British Channel are more desirable subjects for an artist's brush or pencil, than the trim sloops and schooners of the North American coast, which are in fact altogether too trim for his purpose. Not so with the yawl here running before the wind. All is rough and in keeping—the tub-like hull, the burly figures on deck, the darkly-tinted canvas of the sails, the oar doing duty for an out-rigger. On the other hand, contrast, no less than variety, is thrown into the composition, by the introduction of a jaunty gun-brig beating to windward in the middle distance, and the larger men-of-war at anchor on the horizon.

Nor is the scene without local and historical interest. Portsmouth, chief among the naval depots of Great Britain, is visible in the background on the right—or would be, if Photography did not disdain to take notice of objects in the copy set before it, which are rendered without force because partially dimmed by distance. On the extreme left is the anchorage of Spithead, rendezvous and starting-point of many a famous expedition.

For a people insular in position, and maritime by habit and pursuits, the English have not bred many marine painters of eminence—painters, that is, who have grappled successfully with the marvels and mysteries known to "those who go down to the sea in ships." And the remark is made with full remembrance how Turner brought them within the grasp of his daring imagination; how Stanfield, with far less brilliance but with a closer adherence to Nature, married land and ocean in many a rare coast-scene; how that excellent draughtsman, E. W. Cooke, shows himself familiar with the technicalities of shipping, that are a stumbling-block to the uninitiated; how not a few skilful *genre* painters roam the shore, palette in hand, and pick up charming "bits" here and there.

Among the rest, Robins, of London, holds a fair place. He understands his subjects, and composes well. His water-colours are excellent. In this instance, the original is in oil and of large size.

FRANCE TRIUM**PHANT**.

P. P. PRUD'HON.

IN THE GALLERY OF THOMAS J. BRYAN, ESQ.

Very rarely indeed can an oil painting be **persuaded to give back so brilliant a** Photograph as this. The distinctive traits **of the composition, the power and the** beauty, are alike preserved. The exquisite **finish is reproduced. Even the transparent** shadows are not marred **by** any unfortunate **disagreement between the Sun and the** chemical properties of colour. **Can it be that Apollo recognized an obligation to deal sym-** pathetically with certain of his old mythological acquaintances? **It is true, the God of** Day might not have felt much tenderness toward the cannibal Saturn, who is gobbling up one of his offspring in the lower left-hand corner, or toward the inexorable Fates, who are over against him, spinning the thread of human destinies. Yet he could not but have warmed up favourably toward the Muses, and the Sciences, and the winged Minerva, and the lovely bearer of the symbol of Eternity, and the Cherubic boys not destined to the maw of Time, **and** toward what else **there may be of the grand and** the graceful gathered here together in homage to the glory **of France.** Her figure may be easily recognized by her central position, as she sits enthroned **on clouds,** by the *fleurs-de-lys* that bespangle her robe, and by the armorial shield over **which she** throws a protecting arm. Apollo, we say, might have been inclined to greet, **in** this matter-of-fact age, his familiars of the classical long ago; it is certain that **he has not** been discomposed by either varnish or pigment.

Allegory has **gone so much out of vogue, and this work has so many of the splendid** attributes **which we associate with the palmy days of Italian art, that it is difficult to** believe it done by a hand that **was only laid low forty years since. It is either the** original design for a painted ceiling in the city of Dijon, Prud'hon's birthplace, or a highly-finished copy made by himself. **That it was intended for an oblong** ceiling, should be taken into account, in studying **the** grouping and arrangement of the figures. Admirable **as it** is, when viewed in the ordinary way, its fine qualities **are still** more apparent when the eye looks up to, and not down upon it. There are other reasons also —connected with the imagination, and not to be explained in brief space—why allegorical and mythological paintings have been generally limited to the adornment of vaulted roofs. These reasons would **be out of place here; but it may be asked,** whether we would desire to have Guido's **"Aurora," or Annibal Caracci's "Triumph of Bacchus** and Ariadne," transferred from ceiling to wall?

THE GOOD SISTER.

H. MERLE.

IN THE GALLERY OF AUGUST BELMONT, ESQ.

THERE are pictures scattered here and there, **that constrain universal admiration, without stint, and without inquiry into its origin. This is one of them. You recog-** nize forthwith something of the chief excellence **to which painting can attain—an** appeal to the commonest sensibilities of human **nature, happily and irresistibly made.** There is no question as **to** what constitutes the charm ; you **are laid under the spell at** the first glance ; **you surrender** at discretion to its influence.

The **Good Sister! How simple and expressive a** name, **for an expressive and simple subject! Are they orphan children these, that the** youthful **maiden should be thus pre- maturely playing a mother's part ? Is he ill, this sleeping** brother, nestled **so tenderly to her young heart ? Or—as is more probable, in view** of the boy's **chubby face and the bowl beside her—is the nurse's look** sad and anxious, and are the tears ready **to fall from her** eyes, because she knows that henceforth they two **have** only each other upon earth ? The idea is not worth following out ; only, you **feel** assured, by her honesty and earnestness of expression, that so good a sister will never fail to wrestle bravely in the coming battle of life.

Yet, exquisitely touching and artistically beautiful, as is this composition, one would not care to have many such. It is an exception to ordinary rules, and its charm is enhanced thereby ; for, though no age is exempt from sorrow and **suffering, it** is at once more natural and more wholesome that—both **in** sentiment and in art—childhood **should still be associated with joyousness. It is not well to** sadden **one's recollections of the period,**

When the heart danced, and life was in its spring.

Merle is a Parisian ; but it is obvious that there is nothing local in his conception or treatment. He addresses those universal sympathies, **that "make** the whole world kin." If Gallait's historical group of the Duke of Alva and his infamous "Blood Council" be the artistic gem of Mr. Belmont's well-selected collection, it is here, at the shrine of "The Good Sister," that the most frequent pauses are made.

THE SLEIGH RIDE.

W. RANNEY.

IN THE COLLECTION OF WILLIAM H. WEBB, ESQ.

Youngsters, accustomed to the merry jingle of sleigh-bells and **to a rattling pace** behind fast horses, would vote this sober team decidedly slow. **Yet the little urchins,** released from the school-house in the woods, think it apparently **the supremest fun to** mount behind a yoke of oxen, secure however that many an episode **of snow-balling** shall diversify their snail-like progress. **Vividly** indeed has the **painter caught the** exuberance **and the excitement of boyhood, its** sturdy assertion **of individual rights, its** due regard **for the rights of a comrade, its intense interest in the narrow but busy world** **around it.**

The careful drawing of this composition, **and the genial** sentiment **that pervades it,** recall certain familiar acquaintances that German **schools of Art** send hither—and this, though the physiognomies are by no means Teutonic, and **though the** log-hut settles the locality. The artist, in fact, of whom we regret to have **to speak** in the past tense, was an American, prematurely cut off, some few years since, **at the offset** of a promising career. It was in the backwoods of his own country that **he found** his models. The kindly driver, who gives up himself and his ox-cart to **the** entertainment of the playmates, might have stood for his likeness in Vermont or Massachusetts. As for the bright and buoyant **crowd, Young** America is plainly traced in their features.

There **has been occasion** heretofore, **or will be anon, to speak of the inconvenient** caprices of Photography. Here is one of them. **You might wonder why Mr. Ranney** —with many colours open to his choice—should have introduced the violent contrast of black oxen, prominent **as these are, in relief against snowy surroundings. There is no** such contrast in the original. The **sun,** which plays **all sorts of fantastic tricks with the** tints of Nature, is pleased, under this process, to convert red **pigment into black!** Mr. Ranney's colouring is gay, and in harmony with the gaiety of the scene.

THE POACHER.

BRIAS.

IN THE GALLERY OF AUGUST BELMONT, ESQ

It is to be hoped that, in thus designating a picture which is remarkable for its fine drawing and exquisite finish, we do no injustice to the Belgian artist whose work it is, or to the masculine half of the couple whom he has presented. But the truth is, after trying with all diligence to pluck out the mystery of the matter, we have come to the conclusion, that this is not only a case of past poaching on somebody's lands, but of prospective poaching on somebody's household.

For the countenance of the fellow is the perfection of low cunning. His words, doubtless, commend the beauties of the hare which he essays to sell; but his eyes, meantime, by their leer of admiration, extol the charms of her in whom he expects to find a buyer. It is clear that he feels assured of "making his market." The question is—does a deeper purpose animate him? There is no denying that "scamp" is legibly written all over him—in his low, retreating forehead, his coarse jaws, his carnivorous mouth, his mean nose, his squalid form. If also he be an illustration of the saying, that the human face often acquires a resemblance to that of certain animals, it is not difficult to find his exemplar. In the pursuit of his lazy, ignoble, and dangerous calling, the Poacher has acquired, in his expression, something of the craft and cruelty of the wolf.

In speculating, however, upon the question—whether love or lucre, one or both, be prompting the gentleman—it is essential to ponder also upon the aspect of the lady. And it seems to us, that the lady's air and manner betoken a tenderer, or at least a more personal interest than that evolved by bargaining over a hare. It is the Poacher, not the game, that she is eyeing; and, if we interpret her look aright, she is not so much considering the price or the condition of the latter, as the flattering phrases addressed to her by the former. Nor is the surmise to be taken as implying any reflection whatever upon the portly mistress of the kitchen department. She may be prudent, good-natured, industrious, a very pattern of propriety in her sphere; still, the Italian hath it: *la donna e mobile;* and a ruder tongue says more plainly and with much quaintness:

Women they are various
As fish within the sea,
And ten times more precarious
Than spring and winter be.

The accessories in this clever picture are touched with nicest hand.

ANNE OF AUSTRIA'S SHOULDER-KNOT.

ROBERT FLEURY.

IN THE GALLERY OF WILLIAM P. WRIGHT, ESQ.

FEW of the romantic episodes in modern history are more generally known than that piquant adventure of the diamond aiguillette, wherein the Duke of Buckingham, by his far-seeing sagacity and promptness, baffled Cardinal Richelieu, mystified Louis XIII, saved Anne of Austria, and exhibited himself as the very pink of chivalrous gallantry. Here, then, is represented the Queen's entrance at the ball given by the Magistracy, in the Hotel-de-Ville of Paris, where the King had desired her Majesty's presence, and also that she should wear the famous shoulder-knot in question, under belief that by its absence her Majesty's peccadillo would be flagrantly exposed. The ball for reception, it will be observed, took place at noon, as was the custom of the period. There are candles in the chandeliers; but they are not in use. The broad light is the light of day. The comparative simplicity of the hall itself—though well suited for pictorial purpose—will not escape the notice of any one who is familiar with the sumptuously decorated residence of the actual Prefect of the Seine.

The value and the interest of this painting are greatly enhanced by the extreme pains taken by the artist in procuring his material. The principal figures are all portraits, made from well-authenticated sources. The costumes are correct, being absolutely those of the time. A descriptive memorandum, written by the artist himself for Mr. Wright, says of it: "In the centre of the picture is the Queen, followed by her confidante, the Duchess of Chevreuse, and by her Ladies of Honour. She is received by the Provost of the Traders, and by the Civic Officers of the City of Paris. Richelieu, believing that the Queen could not have had either time or means for replacing the love-token that she had given to Buckingham, trembles with rage on perceiving that Anne of Austria's toilette is complete—not a tag is missing. Near the King is his young brother, Gaston, Duke of Orleans, who, being well advised of all the intrigues of the Court, has his eye fixed upon the Cardinal. On the Queen's right, and in the foreground, is a young Lord—the one, without doubt, who had brought back the aiguillette to her Majesty. The Ambassador of Spain, dressed in black, is one of the company at the fête. In the galleries above are gentlemen and ladies of the court."

By an annoying freak of Photography—such as we have had, or shall have, occasion to regret elsewhere—the face of the heroine is the very one that lacks distinctness. It is vexatious to miss her calm, unembarrassed, and quietly triumphant expression. As a work of art, the chief merit here lies in the happy distribution of so many figures, and in the skilful management of the light and shadows.

THE SPARKING OF ICHABOD CRANE.

D. HUNTINGTON.

ALL readers of Irving's "Sketch Book"—and who is not familiar with that humour-ous, tender, playful, picturesque volume?—will remember the quaint "Legend of Sleepy Hollow." It would be difficult to name a more felicitous specimen of the art of story-telling. The outlines of character, slight yet graphic, the skilful arrangement of incidents, the life-like descriptions of natural scenery, the masterly blending of colours and sunshine and shadow, and, withal, the atmosphere of delicate pleasantry encompass-ing the entire narrative—all combine to render it a model story, and to commend it to every one possessing a grain of sentiment or fancy or romantic taste.

The central figures in the Legend are Katrina Van Tassel and Ichabod Crane—figures so clearly made out by the pen, that they lie ready for any painter's brush, and have served as models more than once. Here they are again, and welcome as ever. They are in the kitchen of old Baltus Van Tassel; Katrina, presiding therein after the whole-some fashion of the period, is busily paring apples; and to her—as the old dramatists used to say—enter her swain Ichabod, who has come "a sparking," after the fashion from time immemorial. The artist has localized his persons, with scarce a hint from the original tale. Irving describes the hall, and takes a peep at the best parlour of Van Tas-sel's house; but he does not delineate the kitchen. This, therefore, and the sundry simple and appropriate accessories, are not borrowed from the author's pages.

How closely Mr. Huntington, in putting his figures upon canvas, has followed the pattern drawn to his hand by Mr. Irving, may be determined by a comparison of the Photograph opposite with the lively Legend itself, wherein it is said of the gaunt lover, who shambles in so briskly: "The cognomen of Crane was not inapplicable to his person." "One might have mistaken him for the genius of famine, or some scarecrow escaped from a cornfield."

December and May! Beauty and the Beast! What could Katrina do with such a wooer, but make fun of him—Katrina, who "was a blooming lass of fresh eighteen; plump as a partridge; ripe and melting and rosy-cheeked as one of her father's peaches, and universally famed, not merely for her beauty, but her vast expectations? She was withal a little of a coquette, as might be perceived in her dress, which was a mixture of ancient and modern fashions, as most suited to set off her charms."

XXXII

CAVALIER PRISONERS.

W. CAMPHAUSEN.

IN POSSESSION OF HENRY L. JAQUES, ESQ.

THE absence of colour renders it desirable to **explain whence come** the **strong** flecks of light, that touch so many points in this composition, **and yet are** not balanced by corresponding shadows. And the explanation is **easy**: the sun is low down toward the horizon, his rays glancing obliquely with rich and vivid glow. For the rest, the artist has figured out a scene historically accurate, and at the same time replete with feeling. If he has not put on canvas any special incident, or sketched any familiar personages, he indicates **the Great** Civil War of England, with **its manifold experiences and** teachings. He typifies also a class, in each individual of the group.

They are three and three, these Cavaliers and Roundheads—for surely the tall hound may be counted on the side of his master, without reference to that singular instinct of high-bred dogs which makes them eschew plebeian acquaintances.

And first for the captors. Mark the contrast between the horsemen. What an air of superciliousness, and cant, and conceit, in the better mounted of the two! It may be read on his face; it may be almost seen in his pose, and in the very carrying of his hands. Quite otherwise cast is the bluff trooper who rides **at his side**; entirely different is his expression. He is at home on his hog-maned **pony. The** hand of a wary old soldier is upon his petronel; of a free-and-easy campaigner, on his tobacco-pipe. If his leader be one of the Round-texts of the day, he himself **may be one of** its Ironsides.

So also may a variation be traced between **the** captives trudging a-foot. Both are wounded, as the slung arm **and** the bandaged **head testify**; both march with the resolute tread **of men** who recognize that the fortune of war is against them. But the one in sombre costume is wrapt also in gloomy thoughts. His clenched hand betrays high nervous excitement; and well may he be pondering the fate of his country, or of his sovereign—their past record, or their future chances. His comrade, on the contrary, in the gayest attire of the period, appears by no means overwhelmed at his ill-luck. Many a chirruping word has he for the faithful **four-footed** companion at his side. Come what come may, he is strong in that buoyancy of spirit and that light-hearted carelessness, which are attributed to the Royalists of the day. He could troll a good catch, we warrant, or a ditty anent the coming time,

When the King shall enjoy his own again.

Among the many **good qualities** of this picture, may be noticed the general sense of movement. Turn your head, and you may fancy that Roundheads and Cavaliers will both have passed forward along the shore.

THE BILLIARD SALOON.

VICTOR CHAVET.

IN THE GALLERY OF AUGUST BELMONT, ESQ.

If Meissonier be without rivals, he is not without followers. It is in fact a peculiarity of the modern French schools of painting, that the pupils are apt to attach themselves too obviously to some one of the celebrities of the day. Now it is Couture, now Frère, now Troyon, who sets the fashion; for a fashion assuredly it is. Thus it can hardly be doubted that the brilliant success of Meissonier has induced a taste for oil-pictures on canvas or panel, of minute size, finished with the precision and delicacy that have been long admired on ivory and porcelain, and generally restricted thereto.

Photography is for the most part employed in the reduction, as in the reproduction, of objects. In this instance, it simply transcribes—the size of the original in Mr. Belmont's collection, and of the copy on the opposite page, being nearly identical. As to the subject, the interior of a public Billiard Saloon in Paris might not be deemed a very promising one, even by those who would hesitate to adopt Cowper's sarcastic view of the game itself, as conveyed in the well-known lines:

> Nor envies he aught more their idle sport,
> Who pent with application misapplied
> To trivial joys; and, pushing ivory balls
> Across a velvet level, feel a joy
> **Akin to** rapture, when the bauble **finds**
> Its destined goal, of difficult access.

Just as patient manipulation and masterly touches dignified, in by-gone days, many a Dutch cabaret and Flemish kitchen, so have like appliances here worked out similar effects from material not more inviting. The loftiest subject, that the Muse of History might have supplied, could not have originated more accuracy in drawing, a more harmonious distribution of parts, a more life-like movement, a happier combination of the natural with the picturesque. The Saloon, or Estaminet, is one existing in Paris, and much frequented by Artists. The figures are all portraits. The one smoking a little Dutch pipe is Victor Chavet himself.

XXXIV

THE FISHERMAN'S FAMILY.

W. SHAYER.

IN POSSESSION OF JOHN C. FORCE, ESQ.

SHAYER, it seems, can once in a while quit the hedge-rows of England, and even dispense with that dear old white pony of his—as common with him, as the well-known dappled-grey with Wouvermans. Yet his preference for gentle subjects is still apparent; for, in this coming down from the woodland to the sea shore, the constant toil that makes the fisherman's life a wearisome one is not a feature in the happy scene. Neither do murky clouds remind you that—

> Men must work, and women must weep,
> Though storms be sudden, and waters deep,
> And the harbour bar be moaning—

a disagreeable fact, whereof poets for the most part, and artists not unfrequently, avail themselves, in dealing with this amphibious race.

Indeed, the very reverse may be noted in this genial composition. The old weather-beaten grandsire is evidently amusing his juvenile listeners with a jocose story or a cheery word; and many a work of higher pretension fails to convey, with equal nicety, varying degrees of the sentiment evoked.

Is this a fanciful idea? Look closely. The tiniest of the lot is simply satisfied, content with her privileged place, and too young perhaps to take in the homely point of what is spoken. Next above her is a little one, in whose merriment there is just a grain of doubt. Topping her again is yet another, on whose face the broad grin cannot be mistaken, while the eldest maiden completes the group—smiling but more demure, as though she might have heard grandfather's story before, or as though her thoughts were wandering, even as they will wander at "sweet seventeen."

Was it a purposed contrast? The only grave one of the party is the dog, content like the youngest of his two-footed playmates to be admitted to the family circle, and too well used to the sight of such misshapen fish, as the big one just under his nose, to be moved thereby to any demonstration of curiosity.

THE VIRGIN AND CHILD.

G. MABUSE.

A SHADOWED fac-simile of a picture, that is more than three centuries old, is in itself a curiosity; and the original in this instance must date back beyond 1561—that being the latest period at which Mabuse is believed, by any one, to have been living. Encyclopædists indeed, and biographers generally, set down his death as occurring fully thirty years earlier.

Flemish by birth, this artist was one of the few among his countrymen of that age, who enjoyed what was even then esteemed the privilege of a journey to Italy, and a lengthened communing with the great Italian masters and their works. In what he himself left behind him, there are many traces of an effort to cut adrift from the dry and hard manner that he had imbibed in earliest youth, and to borrow from beyond the Alps something of the delicacy and grace that belonged to a more genial clime, and made its painters immortal. Nor is it difficult to perceive in this composition—a small one, of exceedingly high finish—how local tendencies and enlarged perceptions struggle together into quaint utterance. The blending of early Dutch, with full-blown Italian taste, produces a strange effect.

Possessing ability of the highest order, and highly esteemed by his professional contemporaries, Mabuse was a wretched victim of the fascination of the wine-cup. It is of him that a well-known anecdote is told. Established in the household of a nobleman, as was the custom of that age, he one day received from the steward a valuable piece of white brocade, in order that he might have a new and suitable costume prepared, for the occasion of a visit by the Emperor Charles the Fifth to the house of his wealthy patron. But the brocade was sold by Mabuse, to supply his cravings; yet, nevertheless, he appeared in due apparel. He had made up the article of dress, in paper, and had himself tinted this with such exquisite skill, that only those who knew the scandal were not deceived. What could the Emperor do but laugh, when the fact was explained to him? What the artist, but sink deeper into the mire?

THE SACK OF ROME.

ROBERT FLEURY.

IN THE GALLERY OF AUGUST BELMONT, ESQ

WHICH sack of Rome? The question may well be asked, remembering how many a time the "Niobe of nations" has been the prey of the spoiler:

> The Goth, the Christian, Time, War, Flood, and Fire,
> Have dealt upon the seven-hilled city's pride.

Wide and melancholy indeed was the **choice at Fleury's** disposition; and he has selected for illustration that one among these terrible **scenes,** which surpassed all others in atrocity. It was on the 5th of May, 1527, **that the famous** Constable of **Bourbon,** commanding **three distinct** bodies of German, Spanish, and Italian soldiery in the name of the Emperor Charles V, led the assault upon Rome which ended in its capture and long-continued spoliation, though he himself was killed ere victory had declared for his mercenaries. The character of these ferocious and brutalized legions is well imagined in "The Deformed Transformed" of Byron, where, camped beneath the walls on the evening before the attack, they chaunt a battle-song that reeks with pitiless audacity:

> Oh, the Bourbon! the Bourbon!
> Sans country or home,
> We'll follow the Bourbon,
> To plunder old Rome!

It were needless to point out how the artist has crowded together, upon the Bridge and in front of the Castle of St. Angelo, the ghastly horrors **that** fell thick upon the vanquished. In the tumult and confusion, it is plainly discernible that neither age nor sex nor profession are spared. In the emphatic language of Robertson, in his History of the Reign of Charles V : "whatever a city taken by storm can dread **from** military rage, unrestrained by discipline; whatever excesses the ferocity of the Germans, the avarice **of the Spaniards, or the licentiousness of the** Italians, **could commit, these** wretched inhabitants were obliged to suffer. Cardinals, nobles, priests, matrons, virgins, were all the prey of soldiers, and at the mercy of men deaf to the voice of humanity." Gibbon also says, in his pompous and polished diction, and with one of his frequent sneers at our Faith : "**The** experience of eleven centuries had enabled posterity to affirm with confidence, that the ravages of the barbarians, whom Alaric had led from the banks of the Danube, were less destructive than the hostilities exercised by the troops of Charles the Fifth, a Catholic Prince, who styled himself Emperor of the Romans."

The pen has its poetic license. **Is a corresponding one permitted** to the brush? The anachronism may be slight ; but **the dome of St. Peter's, here** represented, did not look down upon that **marvellous edifice, until more than fifty years after the event** that Fleury has **depicted.**

THE SAILOR'S RETURN.

CARL HUBNER.

IN THE COLLECTION OF WILLIAM H.

SEVERAL times, in these brief notices, there has been occasion to allude to the instinct-ive and powerful domestic sentiment that pervades the vast tract of Central Europe, known by the broad title of Germany. German philosophy may partake largely of mysticism, and German politics may seem to us abstruse and theoretical—but there is no denying that the love of home and its associations possesses the popular mind. Hence the artists of that country consult both their natural tendencies and their interests, in multiplying scenes such as the one before us and others that have preceded it. All the various endearing relations of life furnish subjects in turn; and many a good picture has its ground-work in parental, filial, brotherly, or sisterly affection—apart altogether from that more passionate feeling, which has prompted so much that is noble and lovely in every branch of Art.

In this gladsome composition there is none of the last-named element; nothing subtle, nothing refined. It aspires to no hidden meaning, such as may be traced in that ex-quisite illustration of Schiller's "Song of the Bell," wherein Retzsch has represented the return of the wanderer, whose parents fail to recognize him on his entrance. This is a plain family group, and nothing more. The sailor returns, and is gladly welcomed.

Yet the piece, among its other merits, is by no means wanting in individuality and characterization—two points whereon these delineators of every-day life are fortunately strong, else would they run much risk of repeating each other, if not themselves. There is almost an approach to pious awe in the air and manner of the elder woman, as though her intelligence, enfeebled by age, could scarcely compass the possibility of safe voyages to and from the other side of the world. Note also the mingled satisfaction and pride, wherewith the head of the family eyes his manly first-born. With not a semblance of the old sea-dog about himself, he still seems to be complacently conscious that the young fellow before him is a chip of the old block. Untempered, on the other hand, by any such little foible as this, the doting mother's countenance is suffused with the happiness, amply sufficient to her, of having her sailor boy's hand once more in her own. Fancy may perhaps suggest that the taller maiden, she of the pretty face and self-possessed manner, is not moved to much expression by this arrival, because expecting another in which she has a tenderer interest. At least there can be no doubt that the youngest of the group is thoroughly child-like and natural, in her attitude of wondering curiosity.

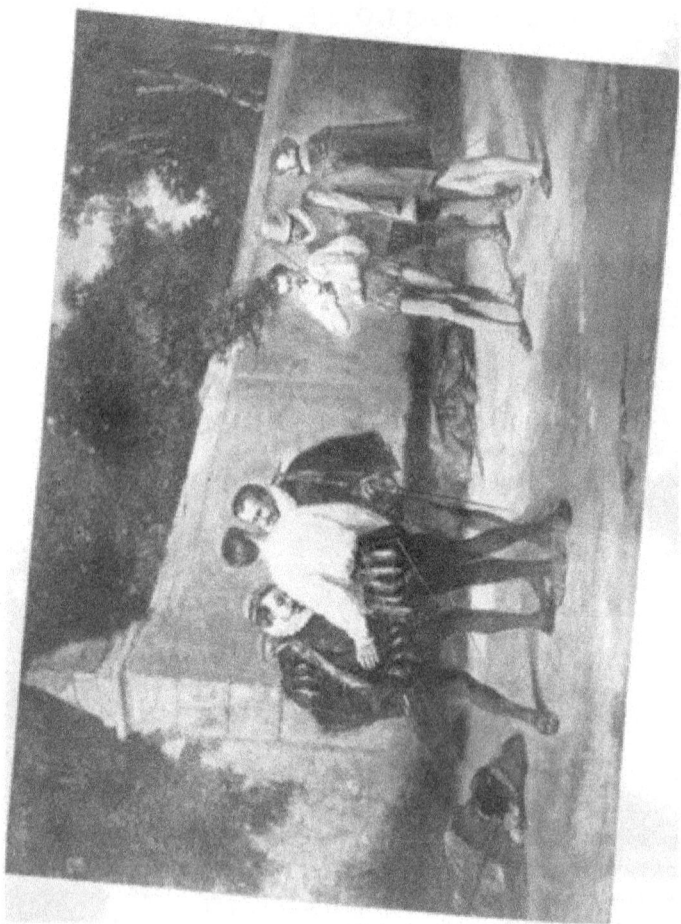

THE DUEL.

J. J. ULYSSE

IN THE GALLERY OF WILLIAM P. WRIGHT, ESQ.

It is not altogether out of **keeping with the gloomy and mysterious** subject of this picture, that the Photograph should come out somewhat **lacking in** distinctness. The side of an old park wall has been the rendezvous, in the **early light of** the morning, as is seen in the lengthened shadows. The men are there in readiness—two, stripped to the **shirt sleeves**, who are the principals; two, on either side, as seconds. There **are no** curious and impertinent spectators. All is **earnest**, quiet, business-like. The period, as indicated by slashed doublet and hose, may be the reign of one of the earlier Henries of France. **There is no mistaking the errand** on which these six grave **personages are met.** The moment of action is at hand—the combatants have cast aside **their heavier garments, which lie there heaped upon the ground, some of** them **possibly destined to enwrap a bloody corpse. They have selected their rapiers, too, and thrown aside the scabbard. One of them, like** *Laertes* **in the play, is examining the hilt of his** weapon, **and perchance exclaims, with that young soldier, "this likes me well."** Coolly awaiting the issue, **he seems to be the very "butcher of a silk button."** The provocation, if one may determine from looks and manner, **comes from the** more distant group.

But whence the quarrel? Not a sign is there of explanation; all is left in doubt on this point. Has the wine-cup or the dice-box, we wonder, brought the two opponents thus face to face? Or are the two gallants about to pit life against life, by way of establishing the relative charms of their respective lady-loves, or by way of ending a rivalry for the same fair lady's favour? Quevedo, you may remember, **contended** that woman was at the bottom of every dispute, as of every crime. **The first one of his pleasant** stanzas **is the key to his suggested mode of fathoming all the mysteries of mischance.**

> 'Tis said a justice of the quorum,
>   Who was no fool,
> When theft or murder came before 'em,
>   Made it a rule
> At once to stop the lawyers' chatter,
>   Saying: D'ye see,
> Let's probe the bottom of this matter—
>   Pray, who is she?

Leaving this **inscrutable secret** to be pondered at the reader's will, we commend this work as entirely **free from stilted and theatrical action.** Duels in our day are, fortunately, seen so much more frequently on the stage than off it, that on canvas they are too generally made to smell of the foot-lamps.

J. PLAGEMANN.

YET a few years, and ships of this class will be no more attached to the Navies of first-rate powers, their places being filled by uncouth monsters clad in metal, which may commit more havoc—with less exposure to their crews—but which assuredly will not gladden the painter's eye.

Here, the eye that took the measure, and the hand that put the likeness upon canvas, were the hand and eye of a seaman, no less than of an artist. Mr. Plagemann, then in the Swedish Navy, saw and sketched the *St. Lawrence* while lying off Stockholm, and subsequently painted carefully, in oil, the original here reproduced. The correctness of detail and proportion shows in truth one sort of professional knowledge, while a foretaste of the other is discernible in the very choice of his subject. A commissioned man-of-war in a foreign port, seen in the deshabille of washing-day, is somewhat shorn of the usual majestic air of force and symmetry combined; but there is great gain on the side of the picturesque. Festoons—even of nameless garments hung out to dry—are more harmonious than the many angles formed by spars and cordage, when the ship is all a-taunt.

A touching little romance—commencing with misplaced love, and ending with premature death—might be made out of the brief career of this young sailor-artist. Three or four years ago, he gave up the naval service of his country, and worked his passage hither, hoping that his easel might earn him a livelihood. His struggle was a hard one. He sketched some, and painted other marine pieces. There was vigour and accuracy in his touch; but there was crudeness withal and the lack of practice. He was not appreciated, and he met with scant patronage. Then—at the beginning of the war between North and South—came a share in the effort to organize here a Volunteer Naval Brigade. The attempt was unsuccessful. Fate seemed to be against him. He returned to Sweden, and died—worn out or broken-hearted, probably both.

XI.

www.ingramcontent.com/pod-product-compliance
Lightning Source LLC
Chambersburg PA
CBHW031454270326
41930CB00007B/994